WORLD THROUGH MY EYES

MY WORLD OF RHYMES VOLUME 1

SMITHA SATYEN

ISBN 979-888503649-8

I would love to dedicate this anthologyto my dearest family and friends

who motivated me and inspired me to pour my thoughts into verses and put

it out before the world.

Contents

Contents

Preface

This collection of poems is just an effort from my side to put before my readers
    my view of the world , my imagination that i have tried to weave into verses.

1. CIVILISATION

Civilisation
Watch how it's become a frustration
Where has it brought us
Is it really a blessing or a curse.
When evolved, it was such a boon
Greed to extremities, made it a bane
Weren't we really better as beasts
Destruction of nature was at least.
Clothes were for pure protection
Today it's just worthless fashion
Hunting was for food or life to save,
Now its down to a cruel game.
Food was to satisfy hunger
Grown from hard toil, sweat and soil
Now it's all artificial and packed in foil
Diseases were few, rare or non existant
Every man today is suffering from ailment
Drugs has made it worse
Just mode of emptying purse
Humans used to live happy , sleep well
Now run from pillar to pole
Trying to achieve irrelevent goals
Tension & disillusion, fear & confusion trying to quell
Just to make their ego to swell

Transport & technology, made life super fast
And death super painful & even faster.
Let's go back to our evolution days,
And finally, put an end to these beastly ways.

2. FRIENDSHIP

First day of school
to be frank, not so cool
scary seemed the world outside home
leving the secure arms of dear mom
every thing seems so different from norm
all new faces with fear & uncertinity torn
there you find a kindered spirit
mirroring on his face your own grith
seeing you sniffle & mourn
he pitches in a wail of his own
together in this alien universe
you embark on a different journey more funnier
apart from all relationship
blooms slowly anendearing friendship
years pass memories grow
some sweet, some deep,
some laced with sorrow
making fun of eachother, pulling legs
snorting to hold back laughter,
while standing to take the pledge
sniggering behind open text books,
when the teacher doesn't look
playing prans on eachother,
sneaking from tiffins during lectures

prompting answers from the back
to bunking classes when one feels the slack
we always stand up for eachother
no matter who be the guilty partner
consoling eachother when we lose our chances
funny nicknamaes are called, however insulting
but coming from your bestie, it's never humiliating
growin older , boasting about crushes
being target of his incessent teasings
yet he's the one to be your messenger
politeness nd formality between you never did exist
whats his is yours nd whats yours ,his
from wolf whistling seeing a pretty head
to smoking your first cigerette
finding a seculded place to get drunk
or just watching the twilight sun in silence
with years our friendship bloomed & blossomed
like wild weeds in the deep rain forests
from sharing our clothes and food
to partaking eachothers happiness & sorrow
when depression strikes nd nothing feels so good
he's the one whose smile you can borrow
no matter how old we still fight like siblings
also shed tears unbashedly watching sloppy films
but when someone threathens either
you stand before him strong ready to fight till death
our parents ,family neighbours
are destiny's favours
but these idiots are mine, each handpicked

thats the true beauty of friendship.

3. THE RACE

The Race

Today I was staring at the sky
I saw the clouds gently pass by
Life before my eyes seem to go
Looking out of my bedroom window
Striving to run my hardest
To find some time to take rest
What am I running after
Some dream that I wish to conquer
I know not what destiny has in store
Still I keep yearning for more
Do I really deserve even this
What I have is already a bliss
Always taking every thing for granted
Is this the life what I really wanted
Sacrifices I had done seem to haunt
Looking in the mirror, my image taunts
You live and breathe, aint that enough
Why making every thing complicated and tough
Look around you ,feel the calm
Concentrate on the next haiku jam..

4. MY HOME; MY HEAVEN

Home
Where my heart is
After exploring the world
Where I find peace
Every corner hold infinite memories
As I sit and stare
The moments spent ,flits by
In my inner eye
My first steps
My moms care
Dad's stern scolds
Fight with my brother
Slowly a tear escapes
Crawls down my cheeks
This I'd not just bricks and cement
But woven out of many a dream
Old dilapidated, paint peeling
Yet the beauty my heart sees
Is unparalleled
My home, my abode, my heaven.

5. METAMOROHOSIS

A lonely Caterpillar green and fat
Crawling on a stalk in despair
Tired of dragging his body around
Sulking in his thoughts without a sound
Saw a beautiful fairy fluttering by
Colorful wings, Oh! what a sight
It watched in awe, mouth open wide
Wish I too were a beautiful butterfly
The more he thought,.more he was sad
Kept on munching leaves to drown the fact
Then finally giving up he wove a cocoon over himself
To hide his plight from the beautiful world
There he lay mourning for hours
Not a morsel of food he did yearn
Oblivious of the change that he endured
Finaly one fine morning
As the golden ray's of the sun hit
The cocoon cracked open by itself
Out of it a dazzling butterfly took a graceful flight
Gliding on his beautiful rainbow wings
Bidding adieu to his past life
decked up for a future merry nd bright.

6. I WONDER !!

I wonder what my future holds
Sometimes how the nature unfolds
How the seasons change so fast,
But when we stare, nothing is changing at all
As a kid we used to wonder aloud
How slowly the time actually passed
Then suddenly we realise, the threshold
Of adulthood we have long crossed
I often wonder how our mind works
Once we were happy with tiny perks
Now even a lot doesnt seen please the mature us
Yesterday was full of laughter and smiles
Todays life is more of tension and strife
What the old age holds in store I again wonder
Will I crib and cry or happily to fate I surrender.
When the final call comes from within
Will it be painful or peace serene
As the soul leaves the body behind
Will I be restless to regain another life
Or float inanother dimension like a feather light
Until I find a new body, new life to begin
Into the womb of my mother a tiny seed again.

7. THE RAIN AND ME

I sit by the window, watching the rain come down
Each and every drop singing its special song
Thunder gongs and lightning strikes
Momentarily illuminating the world outside
My mind weeps for some unknown yearning
The rains does touch my deepest feelings
Memories of lovely past years
Those fun filled times of laughter and tears
Remembering the heart ache, remembering the lost love
Just waiting for someone to pull me out now
I step out into the open, let the rain wash away
Tears or rain water, nobody can say
I kneel to the ground, face buried in hands
Cry all my frustration out,never to be sad again
Let the rain wash away the pain
Let it wash away every sorrow that remain
Slowly the clouds clear, and the sun shines through
Reborn again, here I stand smiling ,person brand new.

8. WONDERFUL WINTERS

Cuddling in blankets,
Staring out of the lancet
Snowflakes showers from sky
Like some rain of sparkling fairy dust
Every thing covered in snow
Like a scenery straight out of a story book
Wafting in air, is tantalizing aroma
Of hot cookies baking in the oven
Laden with butter sprinkled with cinnamon
Making mouths water with temptation
Kids huddled in colorful mitten
Trudging in snow like cute little kittens
Pull on your sweaters and boots
Why waste such weather beautiful
Sitting inside to roost
Get out there, cheeks rosy with cold
Smile broad and bold
Ready to make a giant snowman
With a bowler hat and carrot nose
Have a snowball fight all giggling hard
Or make a snow angel flapping limbs on the ground
Sipping hot steamy coffee freshly brewed

while munching on soft buns mouthful
Thats what maes winter months so beautiful.

9. BE HAPPY

Happy is the heart
who does not care
Doesn't give a damn when people stare
Enjoy every moment, every hour, every day
Forget the past, its gone, future; uncertain
Whatever life hurls, accept with determination
Dont get blinded by the worlds fake charm
Trust your instincts remain calm
Days may differ, seasons may change
Change is the only constant as you age
Happy or sad embrace it with grace
It just add texture to your years
Joyous days and smiles, gives you laughter lines
Melencholy nights gives you frowns and
Tears that cleanse your weary eyes.
Sunshine and spring to give you days of cheer
Lightening and thunder storms help you face your fears
Whatever the situation, however bleak the circumstances
Let the happy smile ,brighten your features
It may give some one hope, or paint someone green with envy
Just be happy ,its not in your hands any way

10. THE SAILOR

Far away in the sea so calm
A lonely figure sailing against the rising dawn
Each gentle stroke of his oar,
The sturdy fisherman pushes his boat
Singing aloud his melencholy strain
Of his little happiness and hurting pain
Loss of his son ,swallowed by the same waves
He holds no grudge for the natures ways
Pride for his pretty daughters
Now married with kids of their own to look after
And of his beautiful wife
Who always stood strong by his side
Now waiting with anxious eyes
For her husbands safe return
He castes his net with a practiced toss
Praying the sea God for enough to cover his loss
Suddenly the sky opens up for a heavy downpour
The rains slashing as the wind roars
He works on paying no heed
He has to fulfill his families need
The angry waves tossing his boat like a rag doll
He puts all his might to gain control,
Slowly the storm passes and calm prevails
He pulls out his nets happy to see a good haul

Slowly he steers his boat ashore
Smiling when he sees her waiting on the shore
Head bowed in prayer for his safe return
She raises her head and meets his eyes
Her own glistning with tears yet smile bright
Slowly she walks up to him on tremblig feet
Together they pull the boat ashore & walk home.

11. DREAMS

Dreams our longings that run deep
Which make our conscience creep
It makes you want to break free
Just leave everything secure and flee
Take a road to destination unknown
Experience every hour as a new born
Bid your family adieu
Take a backpack ,few essentials in tow
Take a friend with you if you could
Or face every thing alone as I should
Out in the vast world where path leads
Meet new people and trust your instincts.
Over the mountains, down the Valleys
Crossing the rivers where its least deep.
Eat when your hungry, rest when you please
Gazing at the starry skies you blissfully sleep
Enjoy every moment let the worries cease.
Travelling on foot or hitch a ride,
Take a boat to cross the tide
Language no barrier, a sincere smile does magic
Use a translator when situation turns tragic
Learn a new custom , listen to folklore age old
Treat your tastebuds to flavours never tasted before
The beautiful earth has lot to offer

Get out there and explore the wonder.

12. ITS WINTER AGAIN....

Open the door, peek outside
Everything is covered in a blanket of white
Tantalising aroma of cookies ,in the oven bake
The snow on roof tops and trees like icing on cake
Snowflakes falling from heaven
Like confetti, sparkles showering in the traven
Cuddle in blankets with hot cup of coffee
Kids waiting expectantly for another toffee
Children bundled up in sweaters coats and mitten
Trudging happily in snow like colourful kitten
Colourful flowers bloom adding warmth
Build a snow man , snow ball fight, skate till you drop
Picnics and parties during winters are a craze
Nothing better than a white Christmas to amaze
When the temperature falls low it turns drastic
But for an outsider the snow is always romantic..

13. BLESSING FROM HEAVEN

Light blue sky stretched far
Weary eyes hopefully scanning
Wrinkled brown hands shading it hopelessly
Sun bearing down its fiery wrath
Bare leafless skeletons of trees
Standing like silhouettes against a white screen
Mother earth parched and cracked
Skeletons of carcass lying abandoned
Vultures circling in search of new feast
Kids in rags, brown dusty faces,
Belly almost sticking to the spine
Trying to forget the hunger pangs
Sad shadow of smile eyes sans sparkle
Engaged in distractions playing with sticks and pebbles
The farmer dejected face, aged with years of toil
Even the tears have dried in the cruel drought
Wails of sorrow, ringing in the back ground
Yet another life has passed on
Escaped from the cycle of hunger & distress
He looks up thanking
One mouth less to feed
His heart cracks once more

Suddenly from afar
A rumble of roars
Hoping against hope he looks up,
Everything is quite in anticipation
Another rumble ,louder this time
Dark clouds gather like a swish of magicians wand
Out of nowhere they fill the sky
Even the children stop playing
Witnessing the magic..
Streak of lightning cracks the sky
Huge drops fall like blessings from above..
The farmers face is a sight to behold
A big smile and tears streaking his wrinkled muddy cheeks
He jumps in a mad dance, singing glory
The children join the ecstacy
Slowly everyone pours out of the homes
Dancing in the heavenly downpour
Mud splattering every where
Evey body is too happy to care.
God has taken sympathy on their woes
Blessed them with eternal hope
After years of scarcity and draught
Finally rain has blessed them all

14. I'M A WARRIOR

I stare into the night, holding fast my wounded heart
The darkness descends engulfing me, making me it's part.
The sound of silence is so deafening
Still it seems weirdly comforting
The crescent moon casting its feeble light
Not enough to fill the void inside.
I Find myself standing atop a cliff steep
Looking down upon the dark rough ocean deep
Stormy winds swirling around trying to sweep,
Into the waiting arms of death waiting abait
Waves crashing as if jeering at my pitiful state.
My cheeks are wet, must be the torrents of rain
Only thing conscious is the soul wrenching pain
No more tears left for me to cry
I have reached the lowest, nothing left to loose, just try
I stare at my fate undaunted in the eye
Though beaten battered and maligned inside
My smile is bright like the sunshine,
Clearing all the clouds of despair,
I promise, I shall rise again
With the armour of confidence and courage
It's now for the world to gauge.
I shall be my soul's saviour
For beware, I am a warrior.

15. UNIVERSE WITHIN ME

I'm the universe
The universe is me
There are no doors or windows
Nor any walls or roof around
You can come, call me
I shall be there for you
No matter, spring or summer
When heaven opens in rain or snow
Sometimes I may be sunny bright
Or gentle as the morning breeze
Sometimes when emotions overwhelm
You can feel the storm brewing
It's up to you to be a part
Or stay away until it blows away
Some are too scared to wander in
Some stay for a while and leave
Many came and then forgot the path
Leaving a little of them with me
Some with their attitude try exploit
Until everything just caves in
Blocking all the path that leads them to me
You are always welcome, in this world of mine

Any time , be it night or day
In my heart forever you can stay

16. LIFE IS TO ENJOY

Winning ..... loosing
Why is it so important
Who sets the parameters
To tag you winner or loser
A top ranking position
Where every moment is a competition
Mouths singing praises
Hiding behind facade of friendliness
Hugging you faking endearment
Just to backstab you at the first chance
No matter how many millions you earn daily
Frustrated you become when accounts don't tally
Beating yourself up for not being worthy
Like your neighbours, relatives or peers
Just peep into their souls for once
They too are shattered with remorse
Hiding behind masks of fake inflated egos
Convincing themselves with false hopes.
No matter how many people praise you
Just one negative comment is enough
To burst the happy bubble
Why doubt your self worth
Why give them the power to hurt
Why put your happiness in hands of others

Close your eyes and look within you
It's your contentment that matters eventually
If you can smile genuinely
Enjoy your life without slaying your conscience
Few hours of peaceful sleep
No regrets whatsoever to keep
Friends true & genuine who doesn't judge
Who's loyalty for you won't budge
Laugh freely ,cry shamelessly,
Travel without boundaries
Enjoy the sun, rains & storms in between
Treasure every pleasure life brings
Forget grudges, Love wholeheartedly,
Be a little weird, be crazy unapologetically
That's what's living life is all about .
Rest all are just illusions, just ignore..

17. EMOTIONS

Random deep and confusing
Sometimes happy sometimes distressing
They just surge within me , unannounced
How shall I deal with I've no clue
I wish I knew how to react
When out of the blue sadness strikes
Lips tremble , heart feel heavy & tight
All I want is hide somewhere and cry
When the sky is cloudy , dark and angry
Everything around seems so gloomy
Inside my heart begins to dread
I know its a forcast for something really bad
No matter how hard I try
I still keep missing the mark
I know not where am I going wrong
Frustrated against this life, being so unfair
When he looks into my eyes
Holds my hand and whispers his love
Thousands of butterflies flutters within me
I become speechless , yet my smile says it all
When my baby adorably smiles
Looking at me with her innocent eyes
I just feel my heart melt inside
Indescribable is that feeling of joy

All I can do is take a pen and scribble
Try to portray them in words feeble
But scarcely could I justify the feeling
For emotions, can't be explained
You really need to thoroughly live it

18. LIFE : DON'T LET IT GO BY.

Life is funny
When we are small
We have dreams impossible
Yet we believe we can do it
We want to travel far
See the whole world & beyond
As we grow up doubts creep in
We lose faith in our own capabilities
The magic which we believed in
So staunchly as kids
We bury it deep within us
Blankatd by heaping reasoning & logic
Scared of being laughed,, being ridiculed
We blindly follow the one above us
Thinking that's the right thing
Coz it is approved by the other's
We see us through others perspective
Obviously thinking we are just not good enough
Finally when wisdom dawns we realise
Life has slipped by, un-applauded
While we were waving empty hands
Trying to catch someone else's dream

The eyes that once wanted to see the world
Now seeks a home ,
No fancy gadgets
But someone to read our mind
Just by looking into our eyes
Someone understands our silence
No expensive luxury, no exotic delicacies
But the lap of mother, food cooked by her hands
If you can accept the moment
Live in it , to the fullest
Love yourself at your worst and your best
Just the way you are now, letting past go
Ready for tomorrow, whenever it comes
You don't need to find happiness
Happiness finds you ...

19. WRITERS BLOCK

I wish I could write

Something really really bright

But now I pity my sorry plight

My words just fail to flow right

I know it's within me

To deal with this mess

But the more I try, it worsens

Leaving me feeling more helpless

I look back on my journey

How far I have come

Going through my own poetries

I wonder, ' did I really pen them!'

I try to calm my agitated mind

Willing to make it understand

Take a break, sit back, meditate

It's just a fog that'll soon clear

It isn't something you can force

Let it take its own course

When the time is right

It will folw beautiful & effortless.

20. NEVER GIVE UP

Every mountain seems huge at first
Every ocean vast and unconquerable
Trust yourself & put your best foot forward
Then another and then another
Before you know you are half way there
Enjoy the journey, it's not the final result
But the entire process that counts
Sailing over the waves, overcoming the storm
It's an adventure that we all have to embark on
When you are tired , almost redy to give up
Sit a while , take a deep breath ,ponder
Look back on what you have achieved
Look within how you have transformed
With a new surge of energy get back on
And before you know the war has been won
Ever trouble in life is a test of your ability
Meant to help you evolve into better
May be others have tried and failed
But you are you, that's your superpower
When your intentions are right, He's with you
He doesn't give the toughest battle
To the strongest warrior
But put the warrior through the hardest
To help him recognise his strengths...

21. YOU'RE INFINITELY BLESSED.

When you think
Nothing's going your way
Life is being unfair
And you don't deserve to be alive
Wait a moment , take a deep breath
Look at yourself, what do you lack
You have a beautiful heart
Pumping blood to every single cell
206 bones holding you upright
Muscles many obeying your will
All your organs working to keep you ticking
Sense organs five, to savour
Everything the world has to offer
And an amazing brain to help you think
You have got this blessing called life
And a beautiful nature that surrounds
Family and friends uncountable
Showering you with love .
Remember this moment too will pass
The darkest night is over
The sun is on its way to brighten the world
So smile your biggest smile

SMITHA SATYEN

Laugh away your fears,
Today is another day to look forward...

22. SCARY MATHEMATICS

Mathematics
Why all these dramatics
The plusses and minuses
Muddling up the senses
The multiplications
Deeper the stress implications
And the mighty divisions
Where the brain ceases to function
The quotient and remainder
Testing my memory power
Makes my imagination wander
Wishing I was somewhere yonder
The time distance and speed
Why not just enjoy the ride
The ratio and proportions
Blowing my mind out of proportion
The sets and Venn diagrams,
It's impossible even to cram
Cost prise selling price, profit and loss
Let the shopkeeper handle the lot
And those inevitable watermelon sums
Who has big hands to handle dozen of them

The area and perimeter
When I buy a field am I gonna myself measure?
Geometry and the theorems
Dumped on the fragile brain cells
After all the fuss of mugging up
You expect us to prove it again
Trinometry torture of another level
The sines and coses and the cosecs and tans
Weren't the English alphabet enough
To rope in the Greeks too into the clan
Poor little X, was so Xclusive and Xtraordinary
In the whrilwind.of mathematics
Completely lost its identity
Always striving to prove its value
Sometimes in fractions or in decimals
Many a times as vulnerable negatives too
Most tortured are the alphabet
When maths invited them into algebra
With its infinite, complex formulas
With its a's & b's and its squares and cubes
Making me want to hunt down
Who ever invented this ruse
It must have been for him a huge breakthrough
But for the poor students it's mental abuse
Fact being that the probability of the probability
Of these in real life ever being used
Is totally, completely almost nil
And us brilliant Indians biggest contribution
That caused nothing less than an revolution

In the field of mathematical universe
But it has become the worst nightmare
Of the poor arithmophobiac student
Being honoured by the sacred ZERO in examination.

23. EVERY LIFE HAS A PURPOSE

A tiny little seed
Within it hides magic
Bury it deep into the dark soil
Watch it slowly grow into a tree
Let the nature nurture it
Showering upon it bright sunlight
Let the rain with its heavenly nectar
Nurture it into life
Let it thrive with the weeds beside
For they too are God's created life
Compete with it for water and nutrition
Tangling roots holding to the earth tight
Braving the harsh summer,
Let the roots go deeper to seek water
Anchoring it more better
Least no upcoming storm dare uproot
Let the autumn work it's magic
Sheding the leaves that has served purpose
Return it back to the soul that nurtured it
Enriching it further for the plant to feed
When the snow covers it in sheets of white
Patiently it bows under the hands of fate

Waiting for the arrival of merry spring
To raise its sleep worn head and blo again
Seasons come and go , years pass slow
Thriving under natures abundance
Fighting adversities growing stronger
Adding it's beauty to the world
You too were a small seed once
Planted in your mothers womb
It's up to you to grow as a pampered garden rose
Or thrive into an enchanting wild flower.
Choose your life you wish to live
Blooming bright, happy, proud and reckless
Wafting your enchanting fragrance into the air
At par with the tiny nose gay or the forest flame...

24. TEA OF LIFE

Life is like tea
you are the chocolate chip cookie
Or any other flavour may be
Just as you dip the cookie
In a cup of hot tea
It depends on how long to keep
Either you get a perfect combination
Of crispy & soft
Or it's still crunchy if not dipped enough
But it may also gets too soggy
If you soak it too long
Yet perfectly melt in your mouth
But if it crumbles in your tea
You get an experience wholly extraordinary
Any way you look at it, it's a win
It's up to you to take it with a salt pinch
With gratitude relish every opportunity
It's your life & so special a blessing
So make the most of it..

25. LIFE IS UNPREDICTABLE

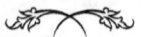

You may have made your plans
All perfectly cut and stacked
That's when life kicks you
Hurling you off your tracks
Throwing you into the unexpected
Sweeping you off your feet
Making you feel quite overwhelmed
And Boom ! You feel the goose bumps
Of the miracle thats manifests
Revealing the hidden potential
You never knew within you existed
Helping you evolve into your bestest
The more enchnted version of yourself..

26. MYSTERY CALLED LIFE

In this journey called life
Many a soul will pass by
There are no strangers here
Just friends, you've never met
Some may just brush past you
Some may walk with you for awhile
Adding smiles sharing joys
Filling your life with light
Each of them will leave on you
A distinct mark of their own
Not all may be pleasant
Not all may with you, kind of gel
But holding grudges isn't wise
For it's not their fault
They're just different
Some may rub you the wrong way
Forgive forget, take it in your stride
For they're just slaves of their situation
Being angry only burns your own peace
Believe in your self & your intuitions
Greet every one with a smile of kindness
Leave a mark of yours on every heart.

27. BEAUTIFUL ANSWERS

When you wish to seek
What you seem to miss
Go back to where you came from
Where all this history of creation began
In the cradle of eternal nature
Which reflects your soul in it's form truest
Not giving you it's opinion or perspective
Neither judging you for your choices
Just guiding you towards answers
Serene and calm in its own elements
Blooming with grace beyond mortal realms
That's where you'll find yourself
You are the solution to every problem
Within you lies the secrets hidden
Waiting to unfold when you focus
Putting all your doubts to rest

28. IT'S GOOD TO BE ALIVE AGAIN

Drizzling rains

Swishing winds

The sun is nowhere

Around to be seen

Summer seems to take a binge

It feels good to be alive again..!!

Droplets falling down the leaves

Going plunge in the puddle beneath

Drawing lazy ripples all the while

Enjoying the merry wether

The birds and bees join the fun

It feels so good to be alive again..!!

Watching through the window panes

As the world goes on its own course

Umbrellas floating around in black & pink

Chattering and giggling kids underneath

Happy to get a chance to soak their feet

Frolic in the showers forgetting everything

It feels good to be alive again..!!

Grown ups are still cribbing

First it was the heat now the rain

Soaked clothes and runny noses

Mud sticking to the toes and heels
Kids getting distracted from their lessons
Trying hard to keep them indoors engaged
But it feels good to be alive again..!!
Fighting my own maladies
I'm getting stronger by the hour
The storm that at night scared me
Now it feels like it's inviting me to dance
Feel the drops cool on my face
Catch it on my tongue and cheek
Breathe in the heavenly petrichor
It does feel good to be alive again..!!

29. BEAUTIFUL NATURE

Dance and music
Nature's way of rejoicing
It is all around you
You just need the vision to see
There is an eternal harmony
In every element of our surroundings
The whispering wind is music
Flowing river ,or the ocean waves
Mighty waterfalls or the gurgling stream
Cacophony of the birds or humming bees
Scampering monkeys or hoof beats of a horse,
Or the fluttering wings as a bird takes off
It's mesmerizing, sort of hypnotising
Drawing you away from the daily humdrum

30. BIRD'S VIEW

Little birdie chirping merrily
Oblivious of the chaos around
Watching the world of humans change
Wondering at the plight they're in
Locked in their houses staring out of windows
Not unlike our caged counterparts
Are they play acting our part
But the dread on their faces aren't farce
Not much smoke emitting from chimneys
Lessened are the honks and beeps
The air too seems less toxic
Water too looks a lot clean
Head bowed down, eyes glued
As if transfixed on the glowing rectangle
Mouth and nose covered by a patch
Moving around from eachothers 6ft detached
Now the silence rents sometimes
By the sirens emitted by a white van
Wails and moans then follow
Scarcely we hear any laughter now
All the animal species totally unaware
Living their life as divinity prescribed
Never meddling with the nature's laws
Silently born serve their due & quietly gone

Why are these bipeds so peculiar
Over dramatizing every phenomenon natural
Poking their nose where needed not
Wrecking havoc and then lamenting to God
How enchanting was this mother earth
Each and every element so divine ,magical
Meandering with its purity making it ugly
Endangering it for yourself & other innocent earthlings
You are just paying for your own sins
Accept your fate and learn what its teaching
So beautiful a life you're blessed with
With your actions you've ruined everything